Diesels in East Yorkshire
Four Decades of Change

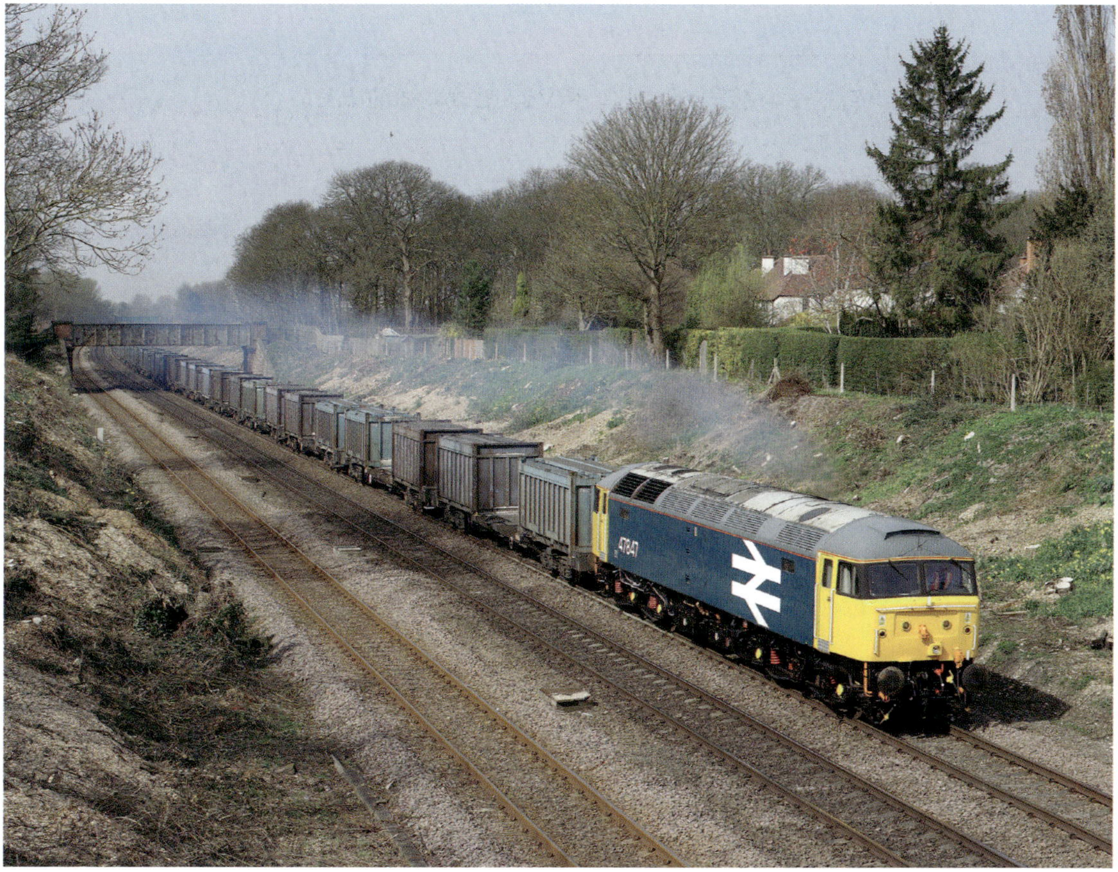

MIKE WEDGEWOOD

KEY Books

BRITAIN'S RAILWAYS SERIES, VOLUME 11

Front cover image: By December 1984 when this picture was taken, goods traffic from Beverley was virtually confined to calcium carbonate traffic for forward distribution to Aberdeen. The goods yard closed with resignalling in March 1985 and this traffic was sadly lost to the roads. This unidentified Class 37 heads south from Beverley in a view that is almost unrecognisable now. Not only has the railway infrastructure altered, but the factory in the background has been replaced by a retail and leisure development and, to the right, a leisure centre and swimming pool have been built. (Eddie Parker)

Back cover image: Imported coal through Hull Docks was regularly seen in the late 1990s and early 2000s, exported coal however was rare. With what looks like a load of export industrial coal, 37521 *English China Clays* and 56051 head a rake of loaded FPAs at Southcoates Lane, Hull, towards the docks on 20 April 2002. (Phil Wheldale)

Title page image: 47847 looks tremendous at the head of 4D94, the 10.23 Doncaster Down Decoy to Hull Coal Terminal empty gypsum containers, as it passes through Ferriby Cutting at 11.28 on Wednesday 8 April 2015. Vegetation clearance on the embankments had recently opened up this location considerably, allowing the spring flowers to add a further splash of colour. (Tony Buckton)

Published by Key Books
An imprint of Key Publishing Ltd
PO Box 100
Stamford
Lincs PE19 1XQ

www.keypublishing.com

The right of Mike Wedgewood to be identified as the author of this book has been asserted in accordance with the Copyright, Designs and Patents Act 1988 Sections 77 and 78.

Copyright © Mike Wedgewood, 2020

ISBN 978 1 913870 38 6

All rights reserved. Reproduction in whole or in part in any form whatsoever or by any means is strictly prohibited without the prior permission of the Publisher.

Typeset by SJmagic DESIGN SERVICES, India.

Introduction

This book, *Diesels in East Yorkshire: Four Decades of Change*, illustrates the fascinating railway infrastructure, stations, signalling, passenger and freight trains in this area over a 40-year period. Using photographs taken by six local enthusiasts, it takes the reader on a journey through the area, showing many of the locations on the railway and the variety of locomotives and multiple units that have appeared from the late 1970s to 2020. Against the backdrop of much steam-age infrastructure and signalling, the resulting photographic journey is an entertaining one!

First a few words of explanation. The journey is from Selby and Goole in the west, to the city of Kingston-upon-Hull and its docks in the east, and then north through Beverley and Driffield to Bridlington, Filey and Scarborough. This makes sense in railway terms but in geographical terms includes parts of North as well as East Yorkshire.

An extract from the North Eastern Railway's tile map of its system that survives at Beverley station shows the significant locations in the area, and the captions to the pictures provide further details about intermediate locations. Some 'then and now' pictures are included to show major changes that

have taken place, but mostly the book concentrates on the trains that ran and the interesting features that once existed throughout the four decades.

The infrastructure of the remaining railways in the area is heavily influenced by the North Eastern Railway (NER). The line from Selby to Hull was opened in 1840 by the Hull and Selby Railway Company, being leased to the York and North Midland Railway in 1845 and then incorporated into the North Eastern Railway in 1872. It is one of the straightest main lines in the country. Built to serve the important docks in Hull, it became a four-track main line between Hessle East and Gilberdyke (shown as Staddlethorpe on the map) in 1904, with marshalling yards for freight being developed in the Hessle area.

At the start of the period covered by this book, significant rationalisation of capacity had taken place in the Hull and Hessle areas but a four-track section remained between Broomfleet and Gilberdyke. In the late 1970s, this line was still mostly mechanically signalled from Ferriby towards Selby; the four-track section was reduced to two in 1988. The section from Melton Lane, just west of Ferriby, to Gilberdyke retained its mechanical signalling until modernisation placed it under the control of York Signalling Centre in late 2018. Throughout most of the period covered, signal boxes at Paragon and Hessle Road Junction controlled the Hull area following rationalisation at Dairycoates, Hessle and Ferriby. This started in the 1960s and continued through to the early 1980s, creating the track layout that is seen in the west of Hull today.

In the Hull area, the origins of the current railway system are a little more complex. The Hull and Barnsley Railway was built in 1885 to provide an alternative route from the Yorkshire coalfields to Hull, but, due to declining traffic, it closed as a through route in 1959. Rationalisation work carried out in 1968, which joined together previously competing routes, means that a short section of it survives as the high-level route. This takes the docks branch from the west of the city to the docks in the east, avoiding the many level crossings that were a feature of city life when the Hornsea, Withernsea and Victoria Dock branches were operational.

As with the Selby and Goole to Hull route, the Wolds Coast line from Hull to Bridlington and Scarborough passes through a rural area and was built by the same company in 1847, again becoming part of the NER in 1872. It was well used and this enabled it to survive a closure proposal in 1968 arising from the Beeching report. Once again the flat nature of the countryside brought an abundance of level crossings and, at one time, there were no less than 39 mechanical signal boxes or gate boxes between Hull and Scarborough. Modernisation began in 1983 but was not completed until 2000; currently there are only five signal boxes remaining.

This railway never had the volume of freight traffic that travelled west of Hull but the seaside resorts of Bridlington, Filey and Scarborough generated significant holiday traffic. While few signal boxes survive, there is a rich inheritance of station architecture with most open and closed stations retaining at least some of their original buildings. Fine overall roofs survive at both Beverley and Filey stations, both of which have been restored in recent years, while that at Driffield was removed to be replaced by concrete awnings in 1949. In this context, mention must also be made of the station at Paragon, terminus to both these railways, and which is a fine NER edifice now serving as the city's rail and bus interchange. Selby and Goole stations also still display much of their Victorian origins.

Amongst the passenger trains serving the area, those to London have always had the greatest status. Operated at the start of the period by a mix of Deltics and Class 47s, in 1980 there were four return workings from Hull to the capital on weekdays. Not forgetting Selby, which at that time, before the opening of the diversion round the new coalfield, hosted East Coast Main Line (ECML) trains from London to Newcastle, Edinburgh and beyond. The Hull services were taken over by HSTs but were reduced over time to one return journey in 1993.

Introduction

This did not meet Hull's needs in full and Hull Trains was created as an open access operator in 2000, running shorter but more frequent services to London. Initially using Class 170 DMUs hired from Anglia Railways and then a purpose-built batch of Turbostars, the service developed using new Class 222 Pioneer sets. These were later replaced by Class 180s transferred from Great Western, and currently new Hitachi Class 802 bi-mode trains. The service has also expanded to seven return journeys to King's Cross, two of which start or terminate at Beverley. One return trip continues to run under LNER operation, now with Class 800 bi-mode units.

The development of local passenger services is also one of growth and expansion. In 1980, the service pattern west of Hull was roughly hourly to Manchester Piccadilly via Sheffield, also hourly to Leeds with some services continuing to Manchester Victoria. Local services also ran from Hull to Brough and Goole, York being served mainly by connections at Selby. At this time, the principal services were operated by Trans-Pennine Class 124 DMUs and similar Class 123 units transferred from the Western Region but, in the mid-1980s, loco-hauled stock replaced them. These operated to Manchester and Liverpool via the Hope Valley, Leeds, Carlisle and York, largely using Class 31s fitted with electric train heat capability. Cost cutting initiatives saw these replaced with early Sprinter units from 1987, while Pacers appeared on local (but still long distance) services around the same time.

North of Hull to Bridlington and Scarborough, the off-peak local service in 1980 was hourly to Bridlington and two-hourly beyond to Scarborough, although more frequent in the peak periods. These were supplemented in the summer by Saturday extras from various parts of Yorkshire. Initially, these extras were mainly loco-hauled, but became DMU operated by 1984. This was with the exception of one remaining loco-hauled Saturday working, which went from Leicester to Scarborough via York, returning via Bridlington and the Anlaby curve to avoid Hull. From 1987, this was operated by West Midlands suburban DMUs until the service ceased on 31 August 1991. That same year, a Hull to Glasgow working ran both ways for holiday traffic using an HST.

Since then, the advent of Sprinter and Pacer units, along with general growth in demand, has led to increased service frequencies but the end of summer Saturday extras. Peak hour extras have always run between Beverley and Hull for commuter traffic, although the number of these has reduced as basic frequencies have increased.

Privatisation has also brought improvements, with Manchester services being provided by the TransPennine Express franchise and local services by Northern. By March 2020, there were two services per hour from Hull to Leeds, with one going on to Manchester Piccadilly and the other to Halifax. There were also more through trains off the Wolds Coast line, the service being half-hourly south of Bridlington with an hourly Scarborough to Sheffield service, together with an hourly Bridlington to York train. There was also an hourly stopping service from Hull to Doncaster.

Class 170s and then Class 185s have worked the Hull to Manchester services and, more recently, Class 170s have returned to provide an improved quality of service through from Sheffield to Scarborough via Hull. Though both franchises have been criticised in recent years, there is no doubt that the local services offered before the Covid-19 pandemic were the best in frequency and train quality that the area has ever seen. At the time of writing, however, services were still operating at a reduced level implemented in response to the pandemic.

Freight services have been relatively few over these four decades, with changes from time to time but always of interest. The start of the period saw traditional railway operation in the Hull area, with pick-up freights hauled by Class 20s running from Hull to Bridlington, coal and other depots in Hull being served by trip workings. A dedicated container service had operated from time to time but did not survive as it ran to a terminal in the west of the city and not into the docks. Chemicals from Saltend were a staple traffic but this ceased in 2002.

The Speedlink and later Enterprise trains catered for a variety of traffic for a time but after these ceased to run, the traffic consisted of block trains. Stone to Dairycoates from Rylstone has run throughout the period, while coal resumed in bulk for power stations and industrial use for a few years, now replaced by occasional biomass workings to Drax Power Station. Steel and gypsum are also regular sources of traffic. At Goole, the docks have seen regular steel traffic and the opening of the Guardian Glass works has brought sand trains from Middleton Towers. At Selby, the Potters terminal has seen Enterprise, intermodal and stone traffic but at present only the latter remains.

While there has never been a huge volume of traffic in recent years, there has been great variety in traction types. The Class 20s, 31s, 37s, 40s and 47s of earlier years are well illustrated here but also continue to visit on special workings, engineers' workings, Railhead Treatment Trains and test trains. More recent years have brought Class 56s, 57s, 60s, 66s and 67s in a variety of colours that characterise the privatised railway. Enthusiast specials have brought strangers to the area such as Class 50s and Westerns plus the return of old friends such as Class 40s and Deltics.

Taken together, all these elements of the local scene combine to give a huge variety of traction types set against a railway, which has retained many of its original features well into the 21st century. Add in the tip-offs from contacts some of my fellow photographers have received over the years and the result is that very few special workings or celebrity locomotives visiting the area have escaped the camera. The outcome is this book, a unique compilation of photographs from an interesting but less known area of the national railway system, which I hope you will enjoy!

Acknowledgements

This is a book I have wanted to produce for some time but it is very much a team effort from a group of friends who are local railway enthusiasts. They are Eddie Parker, Tony Buckton, Phil Wheldale, and Dave Smith, and they have my grateful thanks for use of their photographs and my apologies for what I have left out! Without them, the excellent record of the pre-modernisation railway and comprehensive views of the freight scene in this book would not have been possible. Tony and Phil have also helped with technical aspects of producing this book, including scanning slides, cleaning up the images and assembling them for publication.

I must also thank Associated British Ports (ABP) for permission to publish the photographs taken at Hull Docks by Tony, Eddie and Phil under the terms of photographic permits they held at the time. Several individuals have helped by supplying information over the years, particularly Mick Nicholson and James Skoyles, while local railwaymen have also helped by being friendly and understanding as we have pursued our hobby. Finally, this book is dedicated to Mike Sheriff, part of our group of friends and a lifelong railway enthusiast, who is sadly no longer with us, with thanks for the use of one of his photographs of early diesels in the area.

Diesels in East Yorkshire

Selby

Following the introduction of HSTs on the ECML, the Deltics were generally relegated to semi-fast services. On 3 October 1981, 55014 *The Duke of Wellington's Regiment* arrives at Selby with a York to King's Cross semi-fast. Following the sinking of the Selby coalfield, and the diversion of the ECML, Selby lost its direct services to London but over the last 20 years, and thanks largely to Hull Trains, there were up to eight direct services to the capital each day. (Eddie Parker)

Humble duties for a Royal Train locomotive as 47798 *Prince William* passes Selby at 11.03 on Wednesday 27 March 2002 with the 6D99 Selby Potters Group to Doncaster Enterprise service. This locomotive is now preserved at the National Railway Museum in York. Following diversion of the East Coast Main Line, the through lines visible in the previous picture have been removed. Selby's original station built in 1834 can be seen on the extreme right of the picture; it served as a freight depot until recent times. (Tony Buckton)

47843 *Vulcan* crawls over Selby swing bridge with 4D95, the 15.00 Hull Coal Terminal to Doncaster Down Decoy gypsum containers, at 16.58 on Wednesday 9 July 2014. The 5mph speed restriction over the bridge enables several pictures to be taken of trains crossing it! The station is a listed building, being Selby's fourth station and built in 1891 when the swing bridge was rebuilt in its current position. This locomotive is currently stored unserviceable. (Tony Buckton)

A brand new 66721 backs its load of containers into the Potters Group depot at Selby on 3 June 2006. Trains entering the depot run forward into a long siding next to the main line and then reverse into the terminal, where the locomotive can run round. On leaving, they reverse out into the long siding and then depart. This train, the 01.52 from Felixstowe, no longer runs to Selby, although at the time of writing a stone train still served this terminal. (Phil Wheldale)

Hemingbrough

Preserved 40145 has just passed the old station with Pathfinder Tours' 'East Lancashire Envoy', the 07.15 from Rawtenstall to Scarborough, on a bright 24 January 2004. This was the first excursion to run through from the East Lancashire Railway to the national network via the connection at Heywood. Hemingbrough station closed in 1967, although the other stations proposed for closure between Selby and Hull at the same time were reprieved. (Mike Wedgewood)

Wressle

47787 *Windsor Castle* passes Wressle with the 'North Yorkshireman and Wolds Coast Express', the 06.10 from Bedford to York and then Scarborough via Beverley, on 3 April 2010. This quiet rural station sees few trains call. The station buildings remain but the signal box that used to control the level crossing has been demolished. (Phil Wheldale)

Howden and Eastrington

31451 is seen calling at Howden with the 14.33 from York to Hull on 28 March 1985. At this time, locomotive haulage of such trains was common, although a few years later they were replaced by the new Sprinters and Pacers. Howden has increased in economic prosperity in recent years and the station, although remote from the town, now sees a greatly improved service with regular trains to Hull, York, Manchester and King's Cross. (Mike Wedgewood)

GB Railfreight's 66731 *InterhubGB* is seen at Howden on the rear of the top-and-tailed 11.09 Selby Potters to Felixstowe North intermodal, it crossing over having run wrong line from Selby and heading to Brough to reverse to head for Doncaster. The diversion was necessary due to work on Selby swing bridge closing the normal route. The front locomotive was 66705 and the date 5 September 2014. The signal box remains in situ although now closed. (Phil Wheldale)

On a dull 25 September 1984, 31181 and 31128 double-head the Rylstone to Dairycoates Tilcon stone train as it passes the signal box and wooden waiting shelter at Eastrington. Serving a small village, this station remains open but with a limited service; the waiting shelter has since been replaced and the signal box demolished. 31181 has been scrapped but 31128 remains active on a 'for hire' basis. (Mike Wedgewood)

Goole

60049 stands at the head of its load of sand at the Guardian Glassworks unloading bunker on 6 November 2010. The train, the 04.00 from Peterborough Yard, originated at Middleton Towers and still runs several times a week, although it is now operated by GB Railfreight. The glassworks opened in 2003. Unfortunately, the train now runs at a less desirable time for photographers. (Phil Wheldale)

Goole Docks is a busy port on the River Humber and is bisected by a number of public roads from which port activities can be viewed. Seen on 6 March 1985, 08567 is busy shunting steel in the dock reception sidings amidst the surrounding signal box, semaphore signals and an extensive range of sidings. The distinctive water towers in the background are affectionately known locally as the salt and pepper pots. 08567 remains in use at Eastleigh Works. (Eddie Parker)

Steel trains still run to Goole, although since the previous picture was taken, the signal box and semaphores have disappeared along with most of the sidings. In contrast, the vegetation has increased significantly! Here, 60044 is seen derailed in Goole Docks sidings with the 03.18 Scunthorpe to Goole steel train on 12 March 2016. The derailment was caused by a broken rail and the locomotive was quickly back in service. (Mike Wedgewood)

67014 top and tails with 67028 as they head away from Goole and past Potters Grange Junction with a Railhead Treatment Train (RHTT) on 26 October 2004. It is here that the line to Knottingley diverges. Class 67s were used on these trains in 2004 only, Class 66s being used in 2005. (Tony Buckton)

On 12 February 2013, a spoil heap at Hatfield Colliery slipped onto the track east of Hatfield and Stainforth station. The line did not reopen until the end of July 2013 and rail access to the eastern end of the site was via Hensall with a reversal at Goole. On 24 April 2013, 20302, 20304 and 20312 bring 6Z51, the 06.55 Doncaster Up Decoy to Thorne, into the loop at Goole before running round and continuing their journey towards Thorne Junction. (Phil Wheldale)

31106 passes Goole at 10.41 on Tuesday 8 March 2011 with the 2Q88 Doncaster to Hull, Healey Mills and Drax track recording train. It is seen here running into the loop, used to regulate freight trains if necessary. This loop forms the access to the docks, which also requires use of the adjacent siding. This locomotive is currently located at the Weardale Railway. (Tony Buckton)

On 28 March 1985, 141110 is seen shortly after arrival at Goole as the 12.00 local service from Leeds. These early Pacer units were built to a bus body profile and were narrower than the other Railbus types built subsequently. All of the Class 141s were withdrawn from service during the late 1990s. The station retains its North Eastern Railway character today, despite replacement of the ticket office and demolition of the covered footbridge seen in this view. The Goole to Leeds service has reduced in frequency to just morning and evening services for commuters, although patronage between Knottingley and Goole is light. (Mike Wedgewood)

During major engineering work on Selby swing bridge, the 4L78 11.09 Selby to Felixstowe North was routed via a reversal at Brough before continuing via Goole to regain its booked route at Doncaster. On 3 September 2014, 66725 *Sunderland* **passes under the Fountayne Road footbridge on its approach to Goole station. (Phil Wheldale)**

While there are few major engineering features in East Yorkshire, a second swing bridge exists over the River Ouse at Goole, which 31426 is seen crossing in May 1987 with a Hull to Manchester train. The bridge has been subject to many a hit by ships, indeed 22 times between 1981 and 1991. Most were minor but the bridge was closed for some months after severe damage was caused in November 1988 when the Swedish-registered *Samo* **tried to go through the wrong part of the bridge and got stuck! (Eddie Parker)**

Saltmarshe

55007 *Pinza* passes with the 08.05 King's Cross to Hull service on a bright 29 December 1979. Deltics could often be seen on such services at this time with the arrival of HSTs on longer distance trains. This station, which serves the remote village of Laxton, survived closure threats from Beeching and in the 1980s when closure of the Goole swing bridge was considered. The signal box survived until it was demolished after resignalling in late 2018. (Mike Wedgewood)

Gilberdyke

Shown on the NER map in the introduction as Staddlethorpe, this station was renamed in 1974 to recognise the growth in importance of the village where it is located. On Sunday 19 March 2000, 37799 *Sir Dyfed County of Dyfed* sets back through the crossover at Gilberdyke Junction with a very long rake of Dogfish ballast hoppers, these forming the 8T56 Doncaster to Broomfleet engineers' trip. After setting back, the train worked wrong line to Broomfleet before a reversal. (Tony Buckton)

On Sunday 12 June 1983, 40177 passes Gilberdyke with a return excursion from Bridlington to Manchester. At the time, the section between Broomfleet and Gilberdyke was four tracks but this was reduced to two in 1988 when Gilberdyke station was rebuilt and the lovely old wooden buildings swept away. (Eddie Parker)

31281 passes Gilberdyke with a weedkiller train. The Eastern Region of British Rail operated its own weedkiller train at this time, which was made up of a staff dormitory coach, two stores vans, a spray coach and water tanks. As the train had to cover a wide area, it was observed in East Yorkshire any time from February to September; this one was more logical working in late June 1984. This BR-owned train ceased operation after 1988 when private operators took over. (Eddie Parker)

40033 *Empress of England* approaches Gilberdyke on 3 April 1984 with the Hull to York Dringhouses Speedlink service. On this occasion, it was routed via Goole as it frequently picked up traffic there, amongst which were motor vehicles. (Eddie Parker)

In this picture taken on 10 April 1988, remodelling of Gilberdyke station is in progress with the platforms being extended out over the slow lines and the signals also being repositioned into the trackbed. 150258 is arriving with the 08.52 Manchester to Hull, terminating at Gilberdyke due to engineering work replacing the crossing at Broomfleet, while 150236 is stabled in the siding beyond. These Sprinters worked long distance services such as this in their early days before more suitable units became available. (Mike Wedgewood)

20096 heads the 3S14 11.29 Sheffield to Hull RHTT through Gilberdyke on 29 October 2011 with 20227 on the rear. The annual RHTT season brings a welcome influx of heritage traction into the region, with DRS Class 20s being used since 2006. The exception was 2011 when six non-DRS Class 20s were employed; the others working alongside the two locomotives shown being 20142, 20189, 20901 and 20905 in a variety of liveries. These trains have recently operated to Hull and Bridlington with some workings only reaching Gilberdyke. (Phil Wheldale)

Another RHTT working is seen passing Gilberdyke station but this one is working westbound with the more usual DRS traction. On 10 November 2012, 20312 passes the semaphores at the west end with the 3S14 14.01 Hull to Kirk Sandall working. (Phil Wheldale)

Oxmardyke

On 3 April 1984, 47316 approaches the crossing at Oxmardyke with the Hull to Toton Speedlink service, which mainly conveyed acid tanks from the Saltend works at Hull Docks. Oxmardyke signal box was one of largest boxes on the route out of Hull and, situated between Gilberdyke and Broomfleet, controlled a level crossing over a minor road. (Eddie Parker)

Between Oxmardyke and Broomfleet lies Marr House Farm crossing. The access to the crossing is built out over the former slow line trackbed and provides a good viewpoint to see 180111 passing Oxmardyke's distant signal as Hull Trains' 09.48 King's Cross to Hull service on 25 October 2018. On the other side of the crossing is Broomfleet's distant signal, two such signals at the same location not being a common occurrence on the national network at this late date. Four Class 180 Adelantes started work with Hull Trains in 2008, having transferred from Great Western. (Mike Wedgewood)

Broomfleet

Early morning on 24 May 1984 and 37032 approaches Broomfleet with a well-loaded Leeds to Hull Freightliner. Traffic was not always so buoyant and sadly Hull Freightliner depot was to close before the end of the decade. The major problem was that the depot was on the opposite side of Hull to the port, and containers had to be transferred across the city by lorry. Eventually, the lorries just carried on to the rapidly expanding road network. Freightliner did try to resurrect a service on the docks at the turn of the century but loadings were minimal. This locomotive is now preserved on the North Norfolk Railway, where it still operates regularly. (Eddie Parker)

Broomfleet station is where the last section of four-track railway started, although originally there were four tracks all the way from the Hessle area. In July 1984, 37159 passes the box at Broomfleet with the Hull Saltend to Toton Speedlink service. This locomotive was later renumbered as 37372 and survives in preservation, but is being converted into Baby Deltic D5910 at Barrow Hill. (Eddie Parker)

Broomfleet signal box has developed a more pronounced lean since the previous picture! Dating from 1904, it is a type NE S2 and originally had 60 levers; in its latter years it had substantial support structures at the rear. 66508 passes with a loaded coal train on 21 June 2011. Since the start of the new millennium, Freightliner, DB and GBRf have all operated coal trains from Hull Docks to various power stations, although this traffic has now ceased. (Phil Wheldale)

Cave Crossing

Hull is famed for its Rugby League teams, Hull and Hull Kingston Rovers. The highlight of the Rugby League calendar is the Challenge Cup final at Wembley Stadium, to where fans from all clubs would flock irrespective of whether their club was a finalist. In 1984, the game was between Widnes and Wigan and four special trains ran from Hull. After no doubt a great weekend, one of the specials from the capital approaches Cave on 6 May. For the record, Widnes won 19-6. Cave is situated just east of Broomfleet and this photograph illustrates how close some of the signal boxes are to each other on this section of line, as Broomfleet can be seen behind the train. (Eddie Parker)

On 28 February 2017, 66031 passes Cave crossing with empty gypsum containers from Milford Sidings. The loaded train would later go to Ferrybridge. Cave was the smallest box on the line and, while just a crossing box, had the unusual feature of lifting barriers operated by a handwheel. Apart from Saltmarshe, none of the boxes had been demolished at the time of writing despite resignalling having taken place in 2018. (Eddie Parker)

Crabley Creek

This signal box, just west of Brough, controls a farm crossing and is a very pleasant place to watch the trains go by. Here, 43013 leads the New Measurement Train on its four-weekly visit to Hull, the 08.53 from Derby RTC to Heaton depot, on 13 December 2014. The signal box remains in use after resignalling because provision of a manned crossing is a requirement of the Act of Parliament, which authorised the building of the railway. (Mike Wedgewood)

East Yorkshire has been fortunate with the interesting traction provided for its autumn Railhead Treatment Trains. DRS Class 20s have featured for some time but as their use on other duties has diminished, along with their numbers in service, other Class 20s have been called on to provide support. 20007 leads the 14.44 Hull to York Works with 20205 on the rear at Crabley Creek on 18 October 2018. At this time, 20007 was the oldest main line diesel locomotive remaining in service, having been built in 1957. (Mike Wedgewood)

A change of livery for 66721 compared to the picture at Selby Potters earlier in the book. At that time, it had Metronet colours to mark a London Underground infrastructure contract held by GB Railfreight, but here it now carries a representation of the London tube system and is named *Harry Beck* after the map's designer. Although freight on the lines into Hull is sparse, stone from the Yorkshire Dales has been a regular runner for many years and in the past Classes 25, 31, 37 and 60 have been the regular motive power for the train. The date is 15 March 2017, and the train is 6D72, the 12.32 Dairycoates to Rylstone, seen approaching Crabley Creek. (Phil Wheldale)

Brough

Always a busy station and a calling point for almost every passenger train, 31440 is seen calling on Sunday 14 April 1984 with the 11.00 York to Hull service. It is running wrong line due to engineering work; a guard's van can be seen occupying the other track. (Mike Wedgewood)

On 1 July 1983, 31145 and 31143 approach Brough with the empty Tilcon train from Hull Dairycoates to Rylstone, passing one of the magnificent lattice signals that were still in situ in the 1980s. The Tilcon service still runs, although it is now known as the Tarmac, reflecting a change of ownership. (Eddie Parker)

With a mixture of stock from Virgin Trains East Coast and East Midlands Trains, the 07.00 Hull to London King's Cross departs from Brough on a glorious summer's morning on 31 May 2017. The semaphore is on borrowed time with resignalling work underway along the line. The High Speed Train is one of the most successful trains designed by British Rail in the 1970s but many have now been replaced by more modern Hitachi bi-mode stock, including this East Coast Main Line service. (Dave Smith)

Hull Trains' 802302 is seen calling at Brough on 2 January 2020 with the 11.48 King's Cross to Hull service. At this time, the bi-mode sets were being gradually introduced with some Class 180s remaining in service. Five of the Hitachi units are being used to increase service robustness and frequency. In comparison with the earlier picture, it can be seen that the wooden waiting rooms have been replaced with a more modern structure, although passenger facilities at this busy station remain limited. Brough signal box can be seen in the distance. (Mike Wedgewood)

In 2018, a new vantage point for photographing trains became available with the opening of Ings Bridge, just east of Brough station; this being built to open up land south of the railway for housing and other developments in this sought-after commuter town. On 15 February 2019, West Coast Railways' 57316 leads the 11.23 York to Hull via Harrogate Northern Belle luxury dining train past this location. The Northern Belle is a regular visitor to this line, enabling its passengers to enjoy the rural scenery and views of the Humber Bridge. (Mike Wedgewood)

From the opposite side of Ings Bridge, with a view of Welton signal box in the distance, Europhoenix-liveried 37601 *Perseus* is seen taking imported Crossrail Class 66 PB13 (temporarily numbered 66998) for overhaul as the 13.00 Hedon Road Sidings to Longport on 11 December 2018. The new signalling was in operation at this date. However, Welton's semaphores remained in place with white out-of-use crosses on the arms. (Mike Wedgewood)

Welton

Freightliner's 66623 *Bill Bolsover*, in Bardon Aggregates livery, passes Welton in superb autumn light at 11.41 on Wednesday 20 November 2013 with 4D52, the 10.25 York Yard South to Hull Coal Terminal empty coal hoppers. Welton signal box controls a level crossing on a minor road where the gates were kept closed to road traffic until a vehicle needed to cross. (Tony Buckton)

On 22 January 2013, 66714 *Cromer Lifeboat* approaches Welton crossing with the 6B70 08.00 Hull Coal Terminal to West Burton coal train. Photographs were possible at this pleasant rural location from the field adjoining the railway. However, the Heron Foods distribution centre now dominates the scene here and at Lowfield Lane. (Phil Wheldale)

Lowfield Lane

37672 passes Lowfield Lane with a lengthy 6D51 09.47 Doncaster to Hull Enterprise service on 17 March 1999. This location, just east of Welton, is on a footpath that crosses the railway near the rail entrance to the former Croxton & Garry site. Despite several proposals for rail-based use of this site in recent years, none have materialised. (Tony Buckton)

Viewed from Lowfield Lane crossing, 37058 stands in the works at Croxton & Garry, Melton, after setting down calcium carbonate slurry tanks at 14.20 on Thursday 1 April 1999. The tanks had been conveyed on the Doncaster to Hull Enterprise and were deposited on the outward 6D54 13.56 Hull to Doncaster leg, as there is no access to the site from the west. (Tony Buckton)

On 23 August 1999, 56100 passes the now removed semaphores at Lowfield Lane with the afternoon Enterprise working from Hull Docks to Doncaster. Like many of the locomotives shown in this book, 56100 has not survived and was withdrawn in December 2003 and cut up by EMR Kingsbury during October 2010. (Phil Wheldale)

Would you believe it? In early July 2007, 33103 *Swordfish* passes Lowfield Lane with inspection saloon *Caroline* on a York to York working. While Class 33s used to work cement to York in the 1960s, they are extremely rare in East Yorkshire, probably only ever visiting twice. The saloon, though much maligned by photographers when being propelled, has a fascinating history, once being the Southern Region General Manager's saloon. In 1981, it carried Prince Charles and Princess Diana on the first part of their honeymoon, and in 1982 it had the honour of transporting Pope John Paul when he visited Britain. 33103 is preserved at the Ecclesbourne Valley Railway but no longer operates on the main line. (Eddie Parker)

Melton Halt

On 30 September 1984, 31202 passes Melton Lane with a Hull to Manchester service. The signal box here, situated on Gibson Lane, controlled the level crossing, which had electrically motorised wheeled gates. It also controlled the short three-track section from Ferriby station, which allows faster trains to pass slower ones, particularly stopping trains calling at Ferriby's westbound platform. This locomotive was written off in an accident at Cricklewood in October 1988. (Eddie Parker)

Built by British Rail Engineering Ltd at York in 1986-87, Sprinter 150252 is just two years into its working life as it passes Melton Halt on 26 July 1988 on a Sheffield to Hull working. The halt was primarily for workers at the nearby Humber Portland Cement Company and had one service in each direction per day in the 1980s, being just a footnote in the National Rail timetable. It had just one year left in use in 1988, closing completely on 8 July 1989. The halt and the works are now history. (Dave Smith)

47791 passes the next viewpoint at Brickyard Lane, Melton, at 10:15 on Thursday 29 October 1998 with 6D51, the 08.47 Doncaster to Hull Enterprise service, which on this day would have been a light engine movement had it not been for a one-off consignment of aluminium ingots from Lynemouth. (Tony Buckton)

On Monday 18 February 2002, DRS operated a second train of low-level radioactive waste for export from Hull King George Dock, the waste having originated from Sellafield. The first train had run the previous summer. 20302 and 20303 pass Brickyard Lane, Melton, at 10.30 with the 6Z48 05.57 Carlisle to Hull. (Tony Buckton)

A long lens highlights the fine array of signals at Melton Lane on 4 April 2015. 66230 heads the 4D73 05.45 Drax to Hull Biomass Loading Point. The expected levels of biomass traffic from Hull Docks have never materialised with sometimes several weeks passing between workings. (Phil Wheldale)

Containerised household coal originating from South Wales began working to Hull Docks in 1997, and by 28 April had gained regional headcodes rather than the Z coding of earlier trains. 56049 passes Brickyard Lane, Melton, at 13.33 with the 6M07 Hull Coal Terminal to Warrington Arpley empties, while the loaded train had run as 6E06 from Walton Old Junction. (Tony Buckton)

On 15 September 1979, a Class 124 Trans-Pennine unit passes some lovely signals between Melton Lane and Ferriby with a Manchester to Hull service. When Ferriby box was closed in the 1980s, these signals were replaced by colour lights. As for the unit, while many first generation DMUs were preserved, sadly all these comfortable sets were scrapped. (Eddie Parker)

Ferriby

Saturday March 25 2017 saw 67023 and 67027 top and tailing the 09.14 Derby RTC to Hull test train in place of the usual HST set. It is seen approaching Ferriby at 11.25 in cracking spring sunshine, the freshly applied Colas livery certainly making for a colourful combination. (Tony Buckton)

Ferriby station on 5 June 1978, when the signal box was still operational, sees 40066 pass by with a King's Cross to Hull train formed mostly of air-conditioned Mk2 stock. It may have worked the train from London but, more likely, the Class 40 came on at Doncaster, replacing a Deltic or Class 47. Notably, Ferriby is the last station in the area to retain its wooden station building. Sadly, it is in poor repair so its future is in doubt. (Eddie Parker)

Originally refurbished for operation on non-electrified routes of the abandoned Nightstar project to Europe, locomotives 37601 to 37612 were acquired by Direct Rail Services, a company created by British Nuclear Fuels Ltd to transport Britain's nuclear waste. 37610 *The Malcolm Group* and 37609 pass Ferriby on another occasional low-level waste train, the 05.45 Carlisle-Hull Docks, on 15 August 2005. With the majority of nuclear waste trains then centred around Cumbria, this rare working added to the excitement and variety along the line. (Dave Smith)

Weekend engineering work in the Hull area provided the unlikely Sunday morning sight of DRS trio 37606, 20312 and 20308 on the 6Z68 08.00 Hessle Road Junction to Doncaster Up Decoy. Although the date is 24 March 2013, it was bitterly cold on Ferriby station with a strong wind blowing the light dusting of snow along the platform. (Phil Wheldale)

Hessle

60079 runs along Hessle Foreshore with 6J94, the 12.25 Hedon Road Sidings to Masborough freight depot, on 4 November 2014. In addition to stone traffic to Dairycoates and gypsum to Ferrybridge, steel represents the only other commodity to provide regular freight working into Hull at the time of writing. (Phil Wheldale)

Viewed from the Humber Bridge, 66024 skirts the River Humber on Christmas Eve 2013. At one time a substantial amount of coal was imported through Hull for use at power stations but this has now ceased. The train is the 4D27 06.45 Drax to Hull Coal Terminal formed of HTA hoppers. (Phil Wheldale)

In 2015, a new biomass facility was opened at the Port of Hull to support Drax Power Station's green credentials. The new terminal imports biomass from North America and Europe in the form of wood pellets made of forestry residue from felled trees. The silo can store 1,800 tonnes of product while the automated loading system can load a train with 1,500 tonnes in around 40 minutes. In this view, 66059 is about to pass beneath the Humber Bridge with the 14.21 Hull Docks to Drax biomass working on 6 April 2017. Drax also receives biomass from Immingham, Tyne Dock and Liverpool. The tall structures on the horizon above the end of the train are part of the Siemens wind turbine production facilities at Hull's Alexandra Dock. (Dave Smith)

D1916 (47812) looks amazing on the sweeping curve on the approach to Hessle on the morning of Monday 14 July 2014 with the 4D94 10.21 Doncaster Down Decoy to Hull Coal Terminal empty gypsum containers. GBRf hired Riviera Trains Class 47s from mid-2014 to supplement its fleet pending delivery of further new Class 66s and a highlight of the year was their deployment on freight workings in the Doncaster area, including these gypsum trains to Hull. Four locomotives were employed in this way; Riviera blue-liveried 47815 and 47843, BR large logo blue 47847 and two-tone green 47812 seen here, which was repainted blue during the hire period. This locomotive is still in service with the Rail Operations Group. (Tony Buckton)

170204 in Anglia Railways livery passes through Hessle on 25 October 2001. Hull Trains began operating services to London on 25 September 2000. Initially, Class 170 Turbostar units from East Anglia were used before Hull Trains procured its own Class 170s, which began work in March 2004. These were in turn replaced by Class 222s in April 2005. (Phil Wheldale)

37110 storms through Hessle station on Tuesday 2 April 1985 with a long rake of Presflos forming the T62 trip from Melton Lane to Hessle Speedlink yard. The wagons would return to Earles Cement at Hope running as 7M22 with a 17.12 departure, which ran on Tuesdays and Fridays. In the background, the A63 can be seen under construction and, on the right of the train, the platform canopy was later shortened and the buildings demolished. (Tony Buckton)

On 24 February 2019, a five-coach Great Western HST set, led by power car 43010 and with 43190 on the rear, passes Hessle. The set is on hire to Hull Trains and is working the 12.28 Peterborough to Hull empty stock for driver training purposes. At this time, availability of the company's four Class 180 units had been poor, leading to regular cancellations, and two such HST sets were hired to provide cover. They continued to be maintained at St Philip's Marsh depot in Bristol so required lengthy empty stock trips for maintenance in between regular services to the capital. This picture also illustrates the wide platforms at Hessle; they were extended to cover the former trackbed when the line was reduced from four to two tracks. (Mike Wedgewood)

On 16 November 2017, the Royal Train passes Hessle bringing Her Majesty The Queen to Hull for an official visit, including the new Siemens wind turbine factory. The matching Class 67s are in charge of the train, 67006 *Royal Sovereign* being at the rear with 67005 leading. The picture shows the former station building, which has seen a range of commercial uses since the station became unstaffed in 1989. (Mike Wedgewood)

In this view, GB Railfreight's 66789 passes Hessle with the 11.32 Dairycoates to Rylstone empty stone hoppers on 31 October 2019. This locomotive was formerly numbered 66250, the last of the batch built for EWS, and was one of ten bought from the company by GBRf. It was subsequently named *British Rail 1948-1997* and painted in the BR large logo livery as used in the 1980s. It is always a popular visitor to the area. (Mike Wedgewood)

37710 passes Hessle with the 6E39 Mostyn to Saltend tanks at 09.45 on Thursday 20 July 1995. Industrial action by the train drivers' union ASLEF two days earlier led to the train working at this unusual time, 20 hours later than normal. This locomotive still exists but has been stored out of use for many years at Carnforth. (Tony Buckton)

58006 passes Hessle Haven, just east of Hessle station, on July 29 1997 with the 6Y97 07.25 Milford Sidings to Hull Coal Terminal. Class 58s were never common in the Hull area but did make occasional visits as seen here. This locomotive was exported to France to assist in building new high-speed rail lines and remains there out of use. (Tony Buckton)

60023 passes Hessle Haven on 6 October 1999. A signal box once existed at this point, which was also the junction for Hull Inward Yard. 60023 was stored during August 2008 and is currently languishing in the yards at Toton. (Phil Wheldale)

Just east of Hessle Haven is Hessle East Junction, which gives access to Hull Speedlink yard. Here 37274 is seen with a re-railing train on 29 September 1984. The yard is a small successor to the huge marshalling yards that existed previously, being created to cater for residual freight traffic when the area's infrastructure was rationalised. The signalling and pointwork for the yard were commissioned on 14 August 1983. Today, it sees little use other than for occasional wagon storage. 37274 was converted to 37402 and it remains in service with DRS, appearing at Dairycoates and Beverley in this book. (Tony Buckton)

Dairycoates

The oldest picture in the book, which was taken on 25 August 1968. Hull received a diesel allocation early on as steam was phased out, this including many Type 3s (Class 37), but much less successful was the allocation of Class 14 Paxman diesel hydraulics. These were mainly diagrammed for local trip workings but did not last long. D9543 stands stored with others in the roundhouse at Dairycoates. After barely four years' service, the locomotive was scrapped at Booths in Rotherham just three months later. Others survived longer, for example going to work at Ashington Colliery. (Mike Sherriff)

Charter trains visiting freight-only lines or terminals are an interesting part of the railway scene and here 47839 leads the Branch Line Society's 'Lancashire and Yorkshire' railtour from Manchester Victoria past the remains of Dairycoates shed on 2 March 1991; 47285 was on the rear. It is on the stone terminal's run round loop and, at the time, the former depot buildings were being used by the Humberside Locomotive Preservation Group, custodians of various preserved locomotives. Steam locomotive boilers can be seen to the right of the locomotive. The depot finally closed in 1992. (Mike Wedgewood)

In steam days, Dairycoates shed was one of the largest and Dairycoates West signal box controlled many of the workings. On 10 April 1981, 08777 shunts a single wagon past the signal box. Now the box has gone and there is a single line used only by the (almost) daily Tarmac train from Rylstone Quarry. (Eddie Parker)

On 8 May 1981, 55009 *Alycidon* crosses the flyover at Dairycoates with the morning King's Cross to Hull service. It was a golden age for Deltics to Hull at this time as, since the introduction of HSTs, many of the services were Deltic operated. This locomotive is preserved and has operated on the main line; it can be seen later in this book at West Parade Junction. (Eddie Parker)

37042 and 37698 depart from Hull Dairycoates stone terminal with the late running 6D04 empty Tilcon hoppers to Rylstone, at 13.17 on Wednesday 29 October 1997. Regular Type 3 haulage of this traffic was relatively short-lived under the guise of Trainload Construction, lasting for a period of approximately 18 months from the spring of 1991. By the mid-1990s, Class 60s had been the booked traction for around four years. However for brief periods, pairs of Class 37s would substitute in times of traction shortages or for crew training purposes. (Tony Buckton)

60081 *Isambard Kingdom Brunel* draws forward into the headshunt at Hull Dairycoates stone terminal, on the morning of 14 March 2005, before running round to form the 6D72 empty Tarmac hoppers to Rylstone. This terminal is also accessed from Hessle East Junction. The site of Dairycoates depot was to the right of the locomotive. 60081 was painted in this Great Western green livery, and although it was withdrawn from service with serious engine damage, it has now been bought for preservation. (Tony Buckton)

In recent years, an annual excursion has run from King's Cross to Beverley in connection with a Christmas Carol service at Beverley Minster. On 21 December 2019, 37402 heads the 5Z51 Beverley to Dairycoates where the stock will be serviced before returning to Beverley. (Phil Wheldale)

Hessle Road Junction

37688 brings a set of Saltend-bound empty acid tanks past Hessle Road Junction signal box on 10 May 2001. This was built in 1962 and controls the railway east towards Paragon, west to Ferriby, the Anlaby curve and the docks branch. 37688 is now in private ownership after a spell with DRS, and is currently working for Locomotive Services. (Phil Wheldale)

37116 *Sister Dora* departs from Hessle Road Junction with the 6D54 Hull to Doncaster Enterprise service on 10 May 2001. At this time, the junction for the branch was a single line. The locomotive was unique in carrying this version of Transrail livery and survives in main line use, working test trains for Colas. (Tony Buckton)

Freightliner operates a sizeable fleet of locomotives, particularly Class 66s of various sub-classes, and recently some have appeared in the Genesee & Wyoming livery, the parent company of Freightliner. Here, 66623 is seen on hire to GB Railfreight in return for its 59003 being loaned to Freightliner. It is seen pulling away from Hessle Road Junction, now double track, with the 6D09 10.10 Hull Coal Terminal to Ferrybridge gypsum train on 17 September 2019. Gypsum is used in the production of plasterboard. In recent years, the house-building industry has seen an increased demand for plasterboard, moving away from the traditional sand and cement render. (Dave Smith)

37798 and 37518 are seen here taking the docks branch at Hessle Road Junction with Hertfordshire Railtours' 'Castor and Pollocks' charter, the 07.30 from King's Cross to Saltend, on 26 June 1993. 47819 was on the rear and the tour had already visited Killingholme and Hunslet earlier in the day. 37518 is still in service today with West Coast Railways, but 37798 was scrapped in 2009. (Mike Wedgewood)

'Ghost'-liveried 37717 *Stainless Pioneer* departs from Hessle Road Junction, Hull, at 08.35 on the morning of April 24 1996 with the 6V14 Saltend to Baglan Bay acetic acid tanks. When EWS took over from the three regional freight companies of Mainline, Transrail and Loadhaul, a period of indecision ensued regarding liveries, which resulted in a small number of locomotives being turned out in primer, this being one of them. (Tony Buckton)

Hull Docks Branch

37708 passes Boothferry Park, Hull, at 16.40 on Wednesday 9 April 1997 with a short rake of empty BDAs forming the 6G39 Hedon Road Sidings to Doncaster. The double track section from Hessle Road Junction ends just east of here. This station was opened in 1951 to serve Hull City FC's ground, and a shuttle service operated from Paragon station on match days. It was closed for safety reasons in 1986 and demolished in 2007. Hull City now play at the KC Stadium, which is within walking distance of Hull station. (Tony Buckton)

A scruffy 47060 passes Southcoates Lane on 29 October 1997 with the short-lived 4Z59 Trafford Park to Hull Freightliner. This working had been introduced a few weeks earlier and despite being later extended to Crewe Basford Hall, remained lightly loaded and ceased the following June. This is one of the few photographic viewpoints on the docks branch due to most of it utilising the former H&BR high-level line. However, this section that descends from the former Bridges Junction, and returns to ground level for a short stretch, was installed in 1914 as a connection to the NER lines in the vicinity. (Tony Buckton)

Viewed from Southcoates Lane, 56118 heads the afternoon Enterprise service on 3 March 2003. The brown boxes were part of a short-term contract to move new containers for the Ministry of Defence. Double track has since been reinstated at this point as part of the 2008 improvements to the branch designed to increase its capacity. However, with the loss of coal traffic, there can now be weekdays when no trains traverse the docks branch. (Phil Wheldale)

Viewed from the footbridge, 47975 crosses the Holderness Drain leading the Branch Line Society's 'Humber Navigator II' railtour, the 13.35 from Saltend to Manchester Piccadilly on 13 October 1990. The tour also visited King George dock and Hedon Road sidings, while 47549 was on the rear. At this point, the train is coming onto the trackbed of the former Withernsea branch, which carried straight on behind the train. (Mike Wedgewood)

Hull Docks

Tuesday 1 April 1997 brought the unusual sight of a single Class 37 on a rake of merry-go-round coal hoppers as 37684 *Peak National Park* departs from the EWS train office to Hull Coal Terminal (officially known as Kingston Bulk Terminal) at 10.35 with the 6G44 from Doncaster. The hoppers would be loaded with petroleum coke and depart as the 7Z87 to Rugby Cement at Foxton. The shunter seen in the background is stabled adjacent to the train office, where all workings would pause to deposit the single-line token used to regulate movements over the branch and collect an EWS trainman to pilot the working over the docks system. Despite the appearance of up and down lines at this section, rationalisation resulted in all traffic to the coal terminal and Saltend using the furthest line, while traffic to Hedon Road sidings, the steel terminal or the quays would use the closer line of the two. (Tony Buckton, courtesy ABP Hull)

56006 stands in Hedon Road sidings after arriving with the 6D51 Enterprise service from Doncaster on the morning of January 17 2003. Situated directly to the north of King George dock and approximately half a mile to the east of the security gates, Hedon Road sidings saw something of a renaissance following the reintroduction of mixed freight traffic by EWS. On this particular morning, the train would be split, with the steel sections on the BDA bolster wagons being transferred to No.10 Quay for unloading and the BYA covered coil carriers being destined for Hull Steel Terminal, where the transfer of steel coils from ship to rail would be conducted undercover. The lines visible to the right of the locomotive would be used by bulk trainloads to bypass the yard. This locomotive is preserved at the East Lancashire Railway. (Tony Buckton, courtesy ABP Hull)

37680 looks rather strange with its repositioned air horns while awaiting departure from Saltend Reception sidings at 07.30 on June 5 1998, with the 6V14 acetic acid tanks to Baglan Bay. Situated at the eastern extremity of the docks railway system, the exchange sidings are approximately two miles from the security gates. The cranes that can be seen in the background are connected to the building of a new gas-fired power station, which displaced Marcroft Engineering to a new wagon servicing site nearby. The exchange sidings at Saltend fell out of use when traffic ceased in February 2002, with the remaining wagons being removed the following July. (Tony Buckton, courtesy ABP Hull)

47737 *Resurgent* stands at the entrance to the sidings of BP Chemicals at Saltend on 15 February 2003. It is working the 1Z47 08.18 King's Cross to York 'Crown & Sceptre' railtour, which was organised by Hertfordshire Railtours. 66083 is hidden out of sight at the opposite end of the train. (Phil Wheldale, courtesy ABP Hull)

Just under one mile east of the security gates, 37800 takes the chord to Hull Coal Terminal as it crosses Kingston Terminal Junction at 08.35 on 13 August 1998 with the 6Z83 empty MEA box wagons from Rugby. The loaded return was destined for the cement works at New Bilton (Rugby) and was an approximately fortnightly working for about a year between 1998 and 1999. It usually turned up interesting traction until Class 66s took over in the last few months of operation. 37800 is still in service with Europhoenix. (Tony Buckton, courtesy ABP Hull)

Captured from the opposite side of the line at the same location, 37516 brings a rake of empty and extremely unfamiliar RH Roadstone aggregate hoppers into the terminal at 15.25 on Wednesday 10 March 1999. The train had worked from Toton as 6Z77 to be loaded with a one-off consignment of pumice, which returned as 6Z78 to Allington. The vehicular access road being crossed by the locomotive leads to the sidings known as New Yard, Saltend Reception sidings, and the small wagon repair facility of Marcroft Engineering. 37516 is still active with West Coast Railways. (Tony Buckton, courtesy ABP Hull)

Towards the end of the 1990s, the Enterprise service to Hull Docks ran five days a week, inevitably with a Class 37 or 56. Loading and unloading was normally done on No.10 Quay but a rare excursion to King George Dock North Quay happened on 15 December 1999. On what had been a grey and miserable day, 37673 backed its train into the perfect position when, miraculously, the sun appeared for about 90 seconds, making for a classic dockside shot. The picture is taken looking towards No.1 Quay. (Eddie Parker, courtesy ABP Hull)

Patch-painted 37203 leads 37798 as they pause alongside the Eastern access road with the 6D51 Doncaster to Hull Enterprise service on Wednesday 21 August 2002. The consist has come to a standstill for the train to be split at the entrance to the steel terminal where 09007 (attached at the rear) will propel the BYA steel hoods. The BDA bolsters will continue to No.10 Quay for unloading. Hull Steel Terminal (now known as Hull's All Weather Terminal) was opened on 2 October 1997 and was constructed over a former dry dock and the trackwork leading to No.12 Quay of King George Dock. (Tony Buckton, courtesy ABP Hull)

Thursday 29 April 1999 saw 37248 *Midland Railway Centre* work the 6D51 08.47 Enterprise service from Doncaster to Hull, and is seen in this view shunting lightly loaded container flats on No.10 Quay in a move to make way for other traffic. The train is standing on the trackwork leading to the quayside of Queen Elizabeth Dock, which is served by the cranes visible to the left of the picture. The lines to the right of the locomotive run parallel to the vehicular access road on the quay, and it is these that are normally used for the transfer of various rail-born commodities. 37248 worked on the main line with West Coast Railways before retiring to preservation on the Gloucestershire Warwickshire Railway. (Tony Buckton, courtesy ABP Hull)

56103 *STORA* draws a rake of MEA box wagons forward through the loading pad at Hull Coal Terminal at 15.25 on 24 April 2002. The train would depart as the 6Z84 to Ketton cement works. Despite what the name implies, the terminal has handled various commodities other than coal, including petroleum coke, gypsum and pumice. The storage areas within the compound are supplied by a conveyor system from the south side of No.10 quay, Queen Elizabeth Dock. Saltend Chemical Park dominates the background of this photograph with the gas-fired power station visible on the extreme right. (Tony Buckton, courtesy ABP Hull)

No.10 Quay is well served with trackwork and this view, looking westwards on March 6 2003, shows 09202 adding four BYA steel hoods to the daily Enterprise service. The train is standing on a pair of sidings that include a run-round facility which, due to easy road access and hardstanding, became the normal destination for most traffic requiring road-based lifting equipment. The line diverging to the left is to access the quayside of Queen Elizabeth Dock, while the sheds on the right of the photograph hide the line accessing No.12 quay of King George Dock. (Tony Buckton, courtesy ABP Hull)

56078 *Doncaster Enterprise* looks resplendent as it acts as a super-shunter bringing imported rails off No.10 Quay at 11.31 on 15 October 2003. Rather appropriately, the locomotive had worked in on the daily Enterprise service from Doncaster. The rails would work to Castleton as a direct service later that evening. In this view looking west down the quayside of Queen Elizabeth Dock, a grab used to discharge commodities for Hull Coal Terminal, and the associated overhead conveyor system, can be seen to good effect. 56078 is still in service with Colas. (Tony Buckton, courtesy ABP Hull)

Sporadic importing of gypsum through Queen Elizabeth Dock began in 2002 when the recently founded GB Railfreight won an initial short-term contract. Looking resplendent in the morning sunshine of August 15, 66708 runs in a northerly direction alongside the eastern access road shortly after departure from No.10 Quay with the 4Z50 07.40 to Kirkby Thore. Towards the rear of the train, a stockpile of gypsum can be made out below the conveyor system. (Tony Buckton, courtesy ABP Hull)

St George's Road Crossing

Situated on the main line into Hull, this is one of two level crossings in quick succession. On 14 April 2013, DRS' Malcolm-liveried 66434 stands near the crossing waiting to form the 6Z67 18.30 Hessle East Junction to Doncaster Up Decoy. Extensive engineering work on that weekend also brought 20301, 20302, 20303, 20304, 66302 and 66305 to the Hull area on various engineering trains. (Phil Wheldale)

Anlaby Road Junction

Class 50s very occasionally reached Hull on test after works attention at Doncaster. As far as I am aware, 50037 *Illustrious* on the Pathfinder-organised 1Z46 Scarborough to Swindon 'Yorkshire Venturer' is the only one to make it to Hull on any other type of working. This special ran on 7 August 1988 and was hauled between York, Scarborough and Hull by 9F 92220 *Evening Star*. It is seen here pulling away from Anlaby Road Junction alongside Selby Street. (Phil Wheldale)

Earlier pictures have shown the Network Rail test train that visits Hull on a four-weekly cycle, it is usually the HST or top and tail Class 67s if that is not available. However, on 2 December 2017, neither of these was available and in this view, 37219 *Jonty Jarvis 8-12-98 to 18-3-2005* is seen leading the 11.48 Hull to Heaton test train with 37421 on the rear. It is accelerating away from Anlaby Road Junction, located under the flyover in the background. (Mike Wedgewood)

Engineering works at Whitley Bridge on Sunday 20 July 2014 saw a number of workings run to Hull for a reversal via Anlaby Curve and Hessle Road Junction, before returning to Doncaster. 66561 is seen running alongside Selby Street at 10.08 with the 7Y43 08.30 Whitley Bridge to Doncaster Up Decoy. This was the location of Anlaby Road level crossing, one of 22 in Hull that were recognised as being seriously disruptive to road traffic long before the rise of car travel. A 1950s survey showed it to be closed to road traffic for an average of three hours and 40 minutes each weekday. It was replaced by a flyover in 1964, the vantage point for this picture. (Tony Buckton)

Anlaby Curve

On 31 August 1991, 117306 is working the last booked passenger train, the 12.56 Saturdays-only Scarborough to Leicester, around the Anlaby Road Curve, which connects the Leeds and Scarborough lines. Formal closure procedures for this section of track were needed to enable this service to be withdrawn but the curve remains open for traffic. It had replaced the Hessle Road Junction to Cottingham South Junction line that was closed on 7 May 1965 and was used by trains for the coast route not calling at Hull. (Phil Wheldale)

37194 rounds Anlaby Curve with the 2Q88 Doncaster West Yard to Tees Yard track inspection train, at 07.18 on Tuesday 14 June 2011. 37087 brings up the rear. Both locomotives have since been scrapped. (Tony Buckton)

47851 *Traction Magazine* (ex D1648) takes the Anlaby Road curve at West Parade North Junction with the 5Z65 09.15 Bridlington to Cardiff empty stock on 10 July 2005. At that location on 10 August 1968, the photographer saw the same two-tone green locomotive hauling the 1N49 Bristol to Scarborough. On that date during a three-hour spell, he also recorded: Peaks D59 and D105, Class 40 D398, Class 47s D1538, D1683 and D1824, Class 31s D5538 and D5687, and Class 37s D6713, D6732, D6784, D6788, D6789 and D6835. In addition, D6734, D6735 and Class 20s D8312 and D8315 were seen on the still open docks branch, and D1109 and D6790 on the line into Paragon! (Phil Wheldale)

West Parade Junction

Preserved D9009 *Alycidon* passes Hull Royal Infirmary as it departs with Pathfinders' 'Hull & Leeds Executive' on the morning of Saturday 6 May 2017. Despite the cloud, the matching locomotive and stock make for a fine sight. (Tony Buckton)

Another picture of the Royal Train, this time approaching West Parade Junction pulled by 47799 *Prince Henry* on 8 June 1995. On this occasion, it was bringing Prince Charles on an official visit to Hull. This view has now changed significantly with the old cottages being demolished to accommodate a raised footpath to the KC Stadium, which has been built in the background. This has had the benefit of providing new viewpoints of the railway in this area. 47799 is preserved at Warcop. (Mike Wedgewood)

3 May 2002 saw a visit to Hull of Pacific 4472 *Flying Scotsman* with a Northern Belle charter. The whole train required turning via the high-level line and Anlaby Curve before being dragged back into Hull Paragon. Numerically similar to the A3, 47772 approaches Park Street during this move. The Class 47 remains in service with West Coast Railways. (Tony Buckton)

Hull Station

In this view on 15 June 1979, 03073, complete with match wagon, shunts empty stock. The Class 03 shunters were successful locomotives but the attached wagon was necessary as, due to their short wheelbase, they did not always operate track circuits on their own. In Hull, they were also employed at the Botanic Gardens DMU depot. 03073 is preserved at the Crewe Heritage Centre. (Eddie Parker)

Hull has never been a destination that frequently sees charter trains but over the years some interesting ones have run. Here 45107 and 45007, unofficially named *Phoenix* and *Taliesin* respectively, depart double-headed with Pathfinder Tours' '45 Finale' railtour back to Bristol on 3 October 1987. It had arrived from Scarborough via the Wolds Coast line, having set off from Bristol behind 45106. 45007 was added at Birmingham New Street and then 45107 replaced 45106 at Leicester after it failed at Hinckley, so it was an eventful journey! Neither locomotive survived into preservation. (Mike Wedgewood)

Another enthusiast charter to visit Hull was Hertfordshire Railtours' 'Deltic Reunion', the 08.03 from King's Cross to Hull via Leeds and York, worked by preserved D9000 *Royal Scots Grey*. It is seen running round at Hull on a snowy 2 January 1997. This train was run 15 years to the day after the final BR Deltic-hauled train ran in 1982. (Mike Wedgewood)

97304 *John Tiley* heads the 1Q14 Derby RTC to Derby RTC test train inside Hull on 8 July 2014. Previously 37217, this locomotive was renumbered into the Class 97 series after being fitted with the ERTMS signalling system used on the Cambrian line and is owned by Network Rail. Also known as Hull Paragon, the station is a very impressive building. Opened in 1848, it was extended in 1887 and 1903-05 by the NER and the present arched roof dates from the latter improvement work. In 1933, it had 14 platforms but now has seven; it also houses the bus interchange as well. (Phil Wheldale)

A more recent railtour was the quaintly named 'Luca Pezulla' run by the Branch Line Society, this starting from Lancaster at 06.06 on 20 July 2019. Top and tailed by West Coast's 37669 and Colas Rail's 37521, it first arrived in platform 7 and then shunted across to the excursion platforms where it is seen with 37669 waiting to depart. It is many years since a train carrying passengers used these platforms, although on this occasion passengers were not allowed to alight or board the train. (Mike Wedgewood)

West Parade Junction to Walton Street Crossing

Working wrong line, 20303 and 20301 *Max Joule 1958-1999* enter the worksite at West Parade Junction, Argyle Street, from the direction of Beverley at 11.38 on Sunday 14 April 2013, with a mixed train of sleepers and ballast from Doncaster. The train was one of three that had worked into Hull the previous evening and had spent most of the morning standing (without motive power) adjacent to Walton Street. Work was being carried out to lower the track level beneath the bridge due to clearance issues, hence the drafting in of DRS Class 20s to haul traffic through the worksite. This section of the triangle formed by the Hull to Selby line, Hull to Bridlington route and Anlaby Curve, sees the least loco-hauled traffic, adding to the attractiveness of this picture. (Tony Buckton)

Due to the terrain in East Yorkshire, there are many level crossings. Most cause few problems but as traffic grew in the 20th century, the worst offenders in Hull were replaced with flyovers. Springbank West Road was not so fortunate and today traffic jams there are frequent. The signal box at the crossing was called Walton Street after the road alongside where the famous Hull Fair takes place. In August 1981, 40076 passes the box with the summer-dated Bridlington to Sheffield. Just beyond the level crossing is Walton Street Junction where a single track curve diverges left to meet the docks branch. (Eddie Parker)

47711 *County of Herefordshire* passes the Ideal Standard factory in Hull, en-route from Carnaby to Doncaster, at 12.55 on Sunday 22 February 1998, with the 8T57 spoil trip. Ideal Standard has a long manufacturing history on this site, making central heating and bathroom equipment. Although now split into different companies, possibly its most famous products are the Armitage Shanks range of urinals. (Phil Wheldale)

47971 *Robin Hood* is seen on a track-recording train passing Hotham Road, Hull, on 4 November 1996. At this time, such workings were less frequent than today and the all-over yellow livery for the coaching stock had yet to be adopted. 47971, which was originally numbered D1616, was withdrawn in March 1998 and scrapped at EMR Kingsbury during November 2001. (Phil Wheldale)

Cottingham

A chance visit to Cottingham station on a sunny 1 November 1984 produced this picture of 37126 hauling the daily freight train south from Beverley. The station remains virtually unchanged today, although Cottingham North signal box, seen behind the train in the distance protecting a level crossing, has been relocated to Hull's Streetlife museum. Another level crossing is situated to the south of the station, at this time worked by Thwaite Gates cabin. 37126 was refurbished as 37676 and is still in service with West Coast Railways. (Mike Wedgewood)

Cottingham claims to be the largest village in Britain. It certainly is a bustling place that has a rail service to match it. In normal times there are through services to Scarborough, Sheffield and York and, since the advent of Hull Trains, also to London. On 6 September 2019, 155342 departs with the 13.20 Scarborough to Hull. These units were never common in the Hull area until 2018 when they started to make regular appearances alongside Class 170 units transferred to Northern from ScotRail. (Eddie Parker)

Beverley Parks

66131 is about to pass beneath the Beverley southern bypass with the 6T57 14.00 Beverley to Doncaster on 9 December 2012. Engineering work was taking place north of Beverley with 66054, 66152 and 66164 also in use on works trains. (Phil Wheldale)

About two miles south of Beverley is Beverley Parks level crossing and on 4 March 1980, 20076 passes with the returning pick-up freight from Bridlington. By this time, the train served Beverley, Driffield and Bridlington with traffic including domestic coal, 'whiting' (calcium carbonate), agricultural products, motor shock absorbers and occasional Ministry of Defence traffic. (Eddie Parker)

One of the pleasures of travelling on a first-generation DMU was sitting behind the driver and watching the railway line ahead of the train. Approaching Beverley from the south, it appeared as if the line was going to go straight through the minster before, at the last moment, swinging right. Coming round this curve on 7 December 1979, a Class 47 heads away from Beverley with a Bridlington to Sheffield special. The picture was taken from a footpath stile; stand there now and you can barely see the minster. (Eddie Parker)

With Beverley Minster in the background, 47746 *Chris Fudge 29.7.70-22.6.10* heads the 1Z08 15.30 Scarborough to Whitehaven return charter on 17 June 2015 with 47854 on the rear. A church existed on the minster site from at least the 8th century with the present minster being built between 1220 and 1425. (Phil Wheldale)

Beverley, Flemingate Crossing

Heading south from Beverley on 20 March 1980 is 20215 with the daily pick-up freight. Apart from the magnificent Beverley Minster as backdrop, of particular interest are the allotments that lined the track. Almost certainly these were a leftover from the World War Two 'Dig for Victory' campaign, where every available space was taken up for growing food. These sadly fell foul of health and safety in the mid-1980s and were abandoned. This also aided the annual weedkiller train, which then did not have to avoid spraying at this location! (Eddie Parker)

Perhaps the best known train in East Yorkshire in diesel days was the Saturdays-only summer-dated Scarborough to Leicester service. Taken from the lineside allotments, an unidentified Peak passes Flemingate signal box in June 1984. Before resignalling, this box was one of four in Beverley over a mere three-quarters of a mile. Beverley station signal box can be seen behind the train. (Eddie Parker)

On 18 June 1983, 45027 passes between Beverley station crossing and Flemingate with the Scarborough to Leicester service. At this time, this was very much an industrial area with a chemical works and shock absorbers factory either side of the line; now it has completely changed, as the pictures opposite show. (Eddie Parker)

After being recessed, 31116 sets off back to Hull with the pick-up freight on 19 June 1978. Of particular note at this time were the goods sheds on both sides of the line. The one on the right was later demolished for a road, but the one on the left had a different fate. On Friday 13 January 1984, at approximately 8am, a violent storm hit Beverley. Many properties in the town were damaged but the most dramatic was the goods shed, then used as a bus garage, which was blown down. Fortunately no one was hurt but a number of East Yorkshire buses were destroyed. Most of the rubble landed on the railway but by lunchtime, single line working had been introduced. (Eddie Parker)

On 8 December 1994, 47787 *Victim Support*, the day after being named at London Victoria, is seen at Flemingate crossing with a Leeds to Scarborough Orient Express Christmas lunch special. This luxurious train is occasionally seen away from its usual haunts in the south of England. The view has changed somewhat from earlier years; the signal box and crossing keeper's cottage have been demolished, a leisure centre has been built on the fields beyond, and fine town houses have been built on the right. 47787 remained in service with West Coast Railways, being featured earlier at Wressle, but is currently stored unserviceable. (Mike Wedgewood)

In recent years, a charter train has visited Beverley on a weekend before Christmas to allow participants the opportunity to take part in a carol concert at the minster and to enjoy the attractions of this historic town. Most have been run by UK Railtours with DB Schenker as the operating company and, despite appearances, this one is no different, having departed King's Cross at 08.15 on 21 December 2019. After a Class 90-hauled journey to Doncaster, the train was top and tailed by DRS locomotives 37424 *Avro Vulcan XH558* and 37402 *Stephen Middlemore* for the run to Beverley, and here 37402 is seen departing with the 13.11 empty stock to Dairycoates for servicing. The new road, East Riding College buildings, cinema and retail units on the right mean this scene is much changed from earlier years, although the station buildings and signal box remain. (Mike Wedgewood)

Beverley Station

The daily pick-up freight on the coast line always ran in the morning but the output of the chalk whiting quarry in Beverley sometimes necessitated an additional train. On 20 July 1978, 20010 and 20129 pass Beverley Station Box on route to Hull. The whiting was transported to Aberdeen. After resignalling, Beverley box was the only one to survive in the town, eventually controlling the line down to Hull and north towards Driffield. (Eddie Parker)

Most varieties of first generation DMUs have worked the coast line but undoubtedly the most comfortable were the Swindon Class 123 units, one of which is seen arriving at Beverley on 19 June 1978. Also in the picture is 31116 on the pick-up freight, which was recessed to allow the Bridlington to Hull train to pass. The extensive track layout seen here is now plain double track only. (Eddie Parker)

Resignalling came to Beverley on 17 March 1985 when the semaphores were removed and three signal boxes closed. Just a few days before, an officers' special is seen approaching from the north. The unit is an inspection saloon, formed of DB975539 leading DB975349 and converted from Gloucester Class 100 cars E56101 and E51116 respectively. Also of interest is the home distant signal on the left. Due to the close proximity of the Beverley signal boxes, the signaller in Station box was only able to pull off the starter when a lever had been released in Cherry Tree box. (Eddie Parker)

Passing through the magnificent station at Beverley, on 31 May 1981, is 45056 on an empty stock move. The station is listed and was one of three on the line with an overall roof, the present one here dating from 1908. British Rail carried out significant restoration work on the station in 1990. (Eddie Parker)

Beverley, Cherry Tree Crossing

6 February 1978 was a glorious winter's day and a Class 105 DMU passes Cherry Tree signal box with a Bridlington to Hull service. At one time when planning for resignalling, consideration was given to keeping Cherry Tree signal box open so that the yard it controlled could also stay open. With the reduction in wagonload freight, this did not happen and the yard is now home to a small industrial estate and the local job centre. (Eddie Parker)

By 2 October 1984, most of the wagonload freight had finished on the branch but the chalk whiting quarry at Beverley was still forwarding quite a lot of traffic and, here, 37113 was running round its train prior to heading back to Hull. After resignalling, there was only one crossover left in Beverley and on the odd occasion that it was necessary for a locomotive to run round its train, it meant a journey of 12 miles to the next crossover at Driffield. (Eddie Parker)

Beverley North Crossing

37137 passes Beverley North signal box on 24 August 1978 with a north-bound ballast train. This box used to control the junction of the line to York via Market Weighton until that line was closed in 1965 as a result of the Beeching report. Today, proposals are being considered for its reopening. (Eddie Parker)

The building of the Beverley northern bypass gave another photographic viewpoint, and in this picture 47210 powers away from Beverley with Hertfordshire Railtours' 'North Riding', the 08.33 from King's Cross to York and Scarborough, on 24 May 1997. As with many views around Beverley, the minster is prominent, however the fields on either side of the railway are now a housing estate. (Mike Wedgewood)

Arram

One of the stations proposed for closure by Dr Beeching was Arram, a small hamlet north of Beverley. Yet it survived quite possibly as it lies adjacent to RAF Leconfield, which played a vital role in World War Two; first with Fighter Command during the Battle of Britain and later with Bomber Command. 170461 passes on 3 May 2020 with the 13.01 Scarborough to Hull service; Arram has always had a sparse service but at this time under Covid-19 restrictions, a service was running every two hours, none of which stopped at Arram! (Eddie Parker)

Lockington

This remote station is similar to others on the line, though to a slightly more elaborate design with a portico, which can be seen here. Now a listed building, it closed to passengers in 1960. Sadly it is better known for the collision that took place between a train and a van on 26 July 1986, resulting in nine fatalities. In this view taken on 1 June 1985, Class 108 E54198 leads the four-coach 11.18 Saturdays-only Bridlington to Bradford past the signal box and station. (Mike Wedgewood)

Kilnwick

The line from Beverley to Bridlington runs between the two main routes between Hull and Bridlington so despite being criss-crossed by roads, they are mainly minor so the level crossings cause few problems. One of the loveliest was at Kilnwick with its small crossing box, as seen in March 1985 as a Bridlington to Hull Class 108 DMU passes. (Eddie Parker)

Hutton Cranswick

On 26 August 1985, a Class 37 heads north through the well-kept station of Hutton Cranswick with ballast hoppers. In the 1980s, line capacity was high because of the large number of signal boxes and passenger services more sparse so ballasting could be done if required between trains. Since resignalling and with a passenger service every 30 minutes, such arrangements are impossible so engineers' trains are confined to overnight or line closures. (Eddie Parker)

Driffield

There are few engineering features on the coast line with the only viaduct being a charming small one across the Driffield Trout Beck which, on 17 April 1978, sees a Class 101 DMU on the 11.14 Bridlington to Hull. The trout farmed in the area are as pleasing as this rural scene. (Eddie Parker)

Driffield station had its own delightful gate box. The approach of a train would mean a bell ringing in the station office and out would rush the Porter Signalman – like Perks from *The Railway Children* – who with his wheel would rapidly close the crossing gates. On this very snowy 1 January 1986, a Hull to Bridlington Class 108 DMU arrives at the station. Driffield signal box can be seen in the distance. (Eddie Parker)

Perhaps the shortest ever distance for a charter train as 37042 departs from Driffield on 28 July 1983 with a children's day out to Bridlington. Organised by the Driffield Taxi Drivers, the charity still exists but sadly no longer does the train take the strain. One can only imagine the excitement of the children on their 15-minute journey to Bridlington; maybe some are even reading this book now as adults. 37042 is preserved at Warcop but is unserviceable. (Eddie Parker)

The tradition of holiday trains running onto the Wolds Coast line continued until 1991; seen here is 43059 passing Driffield at the rear of the HST set forming the 10.00 Saturdays-only Glasgow Central to Hull via Scarborough on 17 August 1991. This working happened in 1991 only, although HSTs have worked Glasgow to Scarborough holiday trains in previous years. The track layout is now rationalised, and the goods shed seen on the left of the picture has been demolished and replaced with a small housing estate. Driffield station, seen towards the front of the train, used to have an overall roof but it was removed in 1949 and replaced by the present canopies. (Mike Wedgewood)

Looking from the opposite side of the footbridge from which the previous picture was taken, Wansford Road crossing can be seen. The signal box formerly on the left behind the train had been demolished after resignalling in 1987, but the attractive crossing keeper's cottage remains. Here, 156473 and 156470 pass forming the Sundays-only 12.40 Scarborough to Hull on 19 July 1992. These units were introduced in the late 1980s and were a welcome alternative to the Pacers, which were also seen regularly at this time. (Mike Wedgewood)

Nafferton

Saturday 19 December 1981 was a glorious winter's day with blue skies, sun and snow, while 55002 was due south on the coast line on one of the farewell Deltic tours. Sadly as was common at that time, the tour ran late and 55002 passed Nafferton in darkness. A number of pictures were taken though, including this Class 114 DMU with E56013 leading on a Hull to Bridlington service. The goods shed is still there but now converted into a desirable private house. (Eddie Parker)

The stations and goods sheds on the coast line were built to a very high standard with some like the station at Nafferton almost classical in design. Passing the station and signal box on 3 June 1978 is 37117 on a summer-dated Bridlington to Sheffield working. The box was to close in 1989 but the station is, like others on the line, still well kept. 37117 was refurbished as 37521 and can be seen later on in this book at Seamer and on the back cover at Southcoates Lane. (Eddie Parker)

Lowthorpe

On 28 March 1985, even the signalman at Lowthorpe was surprised when offered this southbound ballast. The photographer was even more surprised as it had been some time since Class 20s had worked north of Beverley and pairs of the Type 1s on the branch were never common. 20083 leads the duo past the signal box. For traditionalists, Lowthorpe was the last place on the branch to retain telegraph poles, though they had gone by 1985. 20083 was later renumbered to 20903 and worked for Hunslet-Barclay on weedkilling trains as can be seen in this book at Filey. It is currently stored out of use. (Eddie Parker)

Burton Agnes

Even after 35 years, the Lockington crash is still raw for many but what few people know is that a very similar accident occurred in 1947 when an army lorry crashed through the wooden gates at Burton Agnes into the path of a Hull to Bridlington train hauled by a D49 steam locomotive. Unlike Lockington, no passengers on the train were hurt, although sadly two army personnel were killed along with ten German prisoners of war. In happier times on 19 June 1983, a Class 37 passes the station with a day excursion to Bridlington. The train is passing the two signal boxes that still remained, though the one in use at this time on the left was demolished in 1995 after resignalling, leaving the older structure, which operated from 1874 to 1903, still in place. (Eddie Parker)

Carnaby

On 19 June 1983, 31227 passes Carnaby with a day excursion to Bridlington. Carnaby had one of the smallest catchments on the coast line and traffic was always light, though the nearby airfield provided a substantial increase in traffic during World War Two. The signal box closed in 1990 and, shortly afterwards, the level crossing was rebuilt a little further west to better serve the old airfield, which by then had become an industrial estate. (Eddie Parker)

Bridlington

By 1984, many of the Manchester to Hull trains were formed of Class 31s and coaches. Frequently during 1984 and 1985 on summer Saturdays, some services were extended to Bridlington. On 24 August 1985, 31455 worked such a service. The train then returned empty stock to Hull and here is pictured alongside Bridlington South signal box prior to departure. This is one of only five signal boxes now remaining between Hull and Scarborough. (Eddie Parker)

66846 passes Bridlington South with the 12.45 Seamer to Doncaster Up Decoy engineers' working, including a Railvac machine, on 20 February 2015. 37219 was at the rear. The track layout is little changed compared to the previous picture but the Colas-liveried Class 66 is a rare visitor to the line. Bridlington South signal box dates from 1893, although the equipment is more recent. (Phil Wheldale)

This picture shows a four-car DMU with Class 108 car E54192 at the rear after arrival in Bridlington's bay platform 6 as the Saturdays-only 08.45 from Sheffield on 29 June 1985. It is taken from the former excursion platforms (7 and 8) and the buildings forming the older part of the station and platforms 1 to 3 can be viewed under the awnings. The station was extended in 1912 to add platforms 4, 5 and 6, with 7 and 8 following shortly after. Currently, only three platforms remain though they are still numbered 4, 5 and 6. (Mike Wedgewood)

20304 and 20301 *Max Joule 1958-1999* are seen at Bridlington after arrival from York Works with a special RHTT working, this running via Sheffield, Barnetby and Goole on 10 October 2008. This year marked the expansion of these services locally, continuing the use of DRS Class 20s and with more services running in daylight. However, when regular timetabled workings to Bridlington did eventually start, they ran in the evening and mainly in the hours of darkness. In comparison to the previous picture, the site of the original station buildings is now a housing estate and the platform awnings have been reduced in length. (Mike Wedgewood)

Continuing the tradition of pre-Christmas railtours to the Wolds Coast line, D1015 *Western Champion* arrives at Bridlington with Pathfinder Tours' 'Yuletide East Yorkshireman', the 05.42 Swindon to Scarborough, on 17 December 2016. The locomotive was running with D1031 *Western Rifleman* name and numbers on one side. Surprisingly, this was not the first visit to Bridlington for D1015 as it worked a railtour to Scarborough on 5 December 2009. As can be seen, semaphore signals remain at Bridlington, these controlling the somewhat complex track layout, which has not yet been rationalised. (Mike Wedgewood)

Flamborough

The railways from Selby and Goole to Hull and Bridlington are largely flat but not so the section from there to Seamer. There is a five-mile climb mostly at 1 in 92 from Bridlington to a summit near Speeton; the climb in the opposite direction from Hunmanby is less severe. A Calder Valley Class 110 power-twin E52077 and E51818 climb past the closed station at Flamborough with the 14.55 Hull to Scarborough on 20 June 1987. Once again it is a listed building, being two miles from the village it serves and closed to passengers in 1970. The line between Bridlington and Hunmanby was singled in 1973 with a signal cabin controlling the level crossing at the date of this picture. (Mike Wedgewood)

Bempton

158793 departs from Bempton with the 10.00 Scarborough to Hull on 12 March 2016. The picture illustrates some of the impressive station architecture still to be seen on the line, all the stations being designed by the same architect, G T Andrews, although to several different designs. Opened in 1847, the station formerly had a signal box and two platforms but the second has been disused since the line from Bridlington to Hunmanby was singled. On an earlier visit in 1986, the lever frame controlling the level crossing gates and signals was located in the front room of the station house, now a private residence. (Mike Wedgewood)

Speeton

144001 is seen at the rear of the four-car 13.46 Scarborough to Hull on 3 October 1987. Both units are in the West Yorkshire PTE livery and were regular visitors, despite being some distance from their home territory. The signal box is shown to good effect and was similar in design to many on the line, being demolished when the level crossing it controlled was automated. (Mike Wedgewood)

Just north of Speeton is Reighton cutting, where an overbridge provides a photographic viewpoint. Climbing to the line's summit through the Yorkshire Wolds on a grey 12 May 1990 are 20010 and 20132 with the quaintly named 'Vladivostock Avoider' railtour. This had originated in Sheffield at 08.56 and was routed via Barnsley, Penistone and Scarborough. It was sponsored by the Class 20 Society and carries two appropriate headboards! 20132 remains active on the main line but 20010 has since been scrapped. (Mike Wedgewood)

Hunmanby

This station marks the start of a double-track section northwards to Filey, which forms a long passing loop to cross trains running in opposite directions. The signal box was built in 1875 and remained operative until 2001 when control passed to Seamer East signal box. Today, both it and the wooden waiting room adjacent have been demolished. In this view, 20902 *Lorna* waits for the road with a York to Hull via Scarborough weedkiller on 23 June 1993; 20903 was on the rear. Just north of Hunmanby, a branch to Filey Holiday Camp diverged at the triangular Royal Oak Junction, it being opened by the LNER in 1947 and closed in 1977. (Mike Wedgewood)

Filey

Two years later and another weedkiller is seen under the fine overall roof at Filey station, while a Class 144 DMU calls on 21 June 1995. On this occasion, the rear locomotive is 20903 *Alison* and the train is working from Hull to York. Filey marks the end of the double-track section from Hunmanby and the roof of the signal box here can just be seen above the train. (Mike Wedgewood)

Gristhorpe

On 29 January 1983, a Class 114 DMU passes Gristhorpe signal box with a Scarborough to Hull service. Gristhorpe controls a level crossing on a minor road yet, apart from Bridlington, it is the only box that now controls any semaphores in the area. A dispute over land ownership meant the crossing automation planned 30 years ago never happened. Of interest at the time, a previous signalman had painted a mural on the box wall of a D49 steam locomotive departing the then open station with a Scarborough service. (Eddie Parker)

Cayton

The station here closed as early as 1952 but the signal box survived as a gate box until closure in June 2000. On 29 January 1983, a Class 110 DMU passes the signal box with a Hull to Scarborough service. Later that year, the line between Filey and Seamer was singled and that, together with the singled section between Bridlington and Hunmanby, has since caused considerable problems, such as when a service runs late or there is a need to run extra services such as a test train. At the time the line was singled, traffic was not at today's level, which is an hourly service in each direction. (Eddie Parker)

Seamer West Junction

On 6 April 2002, 37521 *English China Clays* and 37682 *Hartlepool Pipe Mill* drift down towards Seamer West Junction with Pathfinder Tours' 'Napier Navigator', the 07.22 from Crewe to York and Scarborough. The tour was worked by D9016 to York and from Scarborough wearing its controversial purple Porterbrook livery, explaining the perhaps inappropriate headboard on the Class 37s! 37521 remains operational on the main line today, having worked for Colas and now Locomotive Services, but 37682 was not so lucky; it worked for DRS for a few years but was scrapped in 2016. (Mike Wedgewood)

From the other side of the same vantage point of the A64 road bridge, 142084 is seen climbing away from Seamer West Junction forming the Saturdays-only 08.13 Sheffield to Hull via Scarborough on 3 September 1994. These units often worked longer-distance services for which they were not well suited. Housing development is encroaching on this rural location by this date. (Mike Wedgewood)

An earlier photograph, taken on 10 May 1986, shows 40122 passing the junction with the 'Humber Sceptre' railtour, the return 17.20 Scarborough to Manchester Victoria via York, which had arrived via Bridlington. The public footpath across the junction was a good vantage point for photographing trains at this location, although on occasion, the signalman objected to such practices! Control of the junction passed to Seamer East in 2000, and the signal box and its fine display of semaphore signals were removed. 40122, the pioneer of the Class 40s as D200, is preserved at the National Railway Museum. (Mike Wedgewood)

Seamer Station

Used as an interchange point between services from York to Scarborough and the Wolds Coast line, Seamer had an attractive canopy and buildings on its island platform to suit this role. It is also the second location in this book to show new and old signal boxes still in existence! Seamer East signal box, now simply named Seamer, remains, but the older building seen here has been demolished. 47450 is seen arriving with the 12.53 Scarborough to Holyhead on 4 May 1987. The new bridge taking Cayton Low Road over the railway is under construction at this time and is now a useful photographic vantage point. (Mike Wedgewood)

From the bridge seen under construction in the previous picture, 37087 *Keighley and Worth Valley Railway 40th Anniversary 1968–2008* is seen heading the same test train through Seamer as seen earlier at Anlaby Curve on 14 June 2011. The train had run the length of the Hull to Scarborough line before reversing and travelling back to York. 37194 was the locomotive on the rear of the train. (Phil Wheldale)

Scarborough

This has always been one of the most popular Yorkshire coastal resorts and until relatively recent times, many holidaymakers arrived by train from a wide variety of destinations including Glasgow and Leicester plus from the conurbations found in Lancashire, along with West and South Yorkshire. Consequently, the station was of a size to cope with such numbers of visitors with the necessary infrastructure, at one time having ten platforms plus two excursion platforms outside the main station, the latter closing in 1963. Here 31458 arrives with the 09.34 from Bradford on 15 June 1985. It is passing Falsgrave signal box with its impressive gantry; the sidings accessed by the points on the left were used to stable visiting trains. The trackless bay was platform 1A used by Whitby trains until they were withdrawn in 1964. (Mike Wedgewood)

In 1981, Scarborough's Station signal box was still operational (it closed in 1984) and with its own gantry. From the opposite side of the bridge from which the previous picture was taken, 37087 is seen awaiting departure with a Sheffield train in July 1981 with a Class 40 on a Manchester train. The short distance between the two signal boxes is apparent, together with the length of platform 1, which extends under the bridge. 37087 went on to work for DRS, as seen earlier in this book at Seamer, but has since been scrapped. (Eddie Parker)

Many extras ran on a summer Saturday with a variety of motive power. In July 1981, 40075 awaits departure from Scarborough with a Manchester train and alongside 31235 stands with a pick-up freight. The extent of the station buildings and associated track is clear from this view, including a freight yard in the centre of the town! (Eddie Parker)

In addition to the summer holiday extras, locomotive-hauled trains ran throughout the year on the Trans-Pennine route. Here 45143 *5th Royal Inniskilling Dragoon Guards* awaits departure with the 15.53 to Liverpool Lime Street in distinctly wintry conditions on 22 February 1986. At this date, a Class 08 shunter was retained for shunt-release duties and is seen stabled in the background. (Mike Wedgewood)

By 1991, the Scarborough pick-up freight had finished some years ago but one freight remained. Every three weeks an oil train ran from Stanlow with portions for Harrogate, Boulby and Scarborough. On 26 March 1991, 37430 *Cwmbran* is seen unloading at Appleby's at Scarborough. To access the sidings, the train would arrive at Scarborough station then reverse to the depot. (Eddie Parker)

On 19 July 2007, local enthusiasts were amazed when 47816 traversed the line from Hull to Scarborough with a new bogie cement wagon and test coach. The wagon was on test, but why travel the Wolds Coast line? When asked, a member of the crew said it was because the coast line was a mixture of the good, the bad and the ugly track and if the wagon could make it on the coast line, it could make it anywhere! Since that date, much renewal work has improved the line but even now such engineering trains are restricted to 20mph. Here 47816 is seen ready to depart. It is currently stored out of service at Crewe. (Eddie Parker)